Warning Disclaimer

The information provided in this cookbook is for educational purposes only and is not intended to be a substitute for professional medical advice, diagnosis, or treatment. Always seek the advice of your physician or other qualified health provider with any questions you may have regarding a medical condition. Never disregard professional medical advice or delay in seeking it because of something you have read in this book.

The recipes and nutritional information provided in this book are based on general guidelines for managing diabetes and may not be suitable for everyone. Individual needs and responses may vary. It is important to consult with a registered dietitian, certified diabetes educator, or healthcare provider to create a meal plan that meets your specific health needs.

The author and publisher are not responsible for any adverse effects or consequences resulting from the use of any recipes, suggestions, or procedures described in this book. Use of the information in this book is at the reader's own risk.

THE
CARNIVORE
CHRISTMAS
FEAST

TABLE OF CONTENT

PART I

ABOUT THIS BOOK

Welcome to Carnivore Christmas Feast ——————————— 9

Why Carnivore During the Holidays? ——————————— 10

What to Expect ————————————————————— 11

PART II

FESTIVE APPETIZERS

Introduction ————————————————————— 13

Bacon-Wrapped Scallops ———————————————— 14

Chicken Liver Pâté ————————————————— 16

Beef Tartare ——————————————————————— 18

Hard Cheese and Meat Platter ——————————————— 20

Grilled Shrimp Skewers ————————————————— 22

PART III

HEARTY SOUPS AND STEWS

Introduction ————————————————————— 25

Beef Bone Broth ——————————————————— 26

Creamy Chicken Soup ————————————————— 28

Pork Belly Stew ——————————————————— 30

Lamb Shank Stew ——————————————————— 32

Fish Broth with Sardines ————————————————— 34

PART IV

SHOW-STOPPING MAIN COURSES

Introduction ———————————————————————— 37

Roast Prime Rib ——————————————————————— 38

Glazed Ham (Carnivore Style) ———————————————— 40

Roast Turkey with Herb Butter ————————————————— 42

Rack of Lamb ———————————————————————— 44

Carnivore Meatloaf —————————————————————— 46

PART V

FESTIVE SIDES

Introduction ———————————————————————— 49

Butter-Basted Shrimp ————————————————————— 50

Cheesy Egg Bake ——————————————————————— 52

Carnivore Sausage Rolls ———————————————————— 54

Stuffed Pork Loin ——————————————————————— 56

Beef Fat Roasted Bones ———————————————————— 58

PART VI

DELECTABLE DESSERTS

Introduction ———————————————————————— 61

Carnivore Cheesecake ————————————————————— 62

Eggnog Pudding ——————————————————————— 64

Butter and Cheese Fat Bombs ————————————————— 66

Frozen Cream Bites —————————————————————— 68

Carnivore Custard ——————————————————————— 70

PART VII

CARNIVORE-FRIENDLY BEVERAGES

Introduction —————————————————————— 73

Bone Broth Latte ——————————————————— 74

Carnivore Eggnog ——————————————————— 76

Butter Coffee ————————————————————— 78

Carnivore Milkshake —————————————————— 80

Meat Stock Tea ———————————————————— 82

PART VIII

CONCLUSION

Tips for Traveling During the Holidays ————————— 85

Carnivore Shopping List —————————————————— 86

Resources ——————————————————————— 87

Thank you ——————————————————————— 88

PART I

ABOUT THIS BOOK

The holiday season is a time of joy, celebration, and togetherness, often centered around bountiful meals shared with family and friends. For those who follow a carnivore diet, however, navigating the festive season can present unique challenges. Traditional holiday feasts are often laden with plant-based sides, sugary desserts, and carb-heavy dishes that don't align with the principles of a meat-based diet. But with the right approach, the holidays can still be a time of indulgence and delight without straying from your carnivore lifestyle.

In this book, **"Carnivore Christmas Feast,"** we've crafted a collection of delicious, festive recipes that adhere strictly to the carnivore diet—eliminating all plant foods and focusing solely on nutrient-dense animal products. This guide will help you embrace the holiday spirit while staying true to your dietary commitments.

WHY CARNIVORE DURING THE HOLIDAYS?

Following a carnivore diet during the holidays offers a host of benefits, from maintaining steady energy levels to avoiding the pitfalls of sugar-induced crashes that are all too common during this time of year. By sticking to a diet rich in animal-based foods like beef, chicken, pork, fish, eggs, and small amounts of low-lactose dairy, you're not only supporting your health but also enjoying meals that are satisfying and deeply nourishing.

Moreover, a carnivore diet simplifies holiday cooking. Instead of juggling a multitude of ingredients and dishes, you can focus on preparing a few, high-quality meat-centric courses that will leave your guests—whether they follow a carnivore diet or not—impressed and satiated.

This book is your ultimate guide to enjoying a carnivore Christmas. From mouth-watering appetizers to show-stopping main courses, hearty soups, and even carnivore-friendly desserts, you'll find recipes that are both festive and fully compliant with the carnivore diet. We've also included practical tips for navigating holiday gatherings, meal planning, and even traveling while maintaining your diet.

Whether you're hosting a large family gathering, attending a holiday potluck, or simply enjoying a quiet Christmas at home, "Carnivore Christmas Feast" will ensure your holiday meals are joyous, flavorful, and entirely carnivore.

Let's dive into the joy of holiday cooking—carnivore style!

PART II

FESTIVE APPETIZERS

Appetizers are much more than the first course; they're sort of the opening act that's going to set the stage for everything else to follow. In a holiday environment—already primed for indulgence and celebratory excess—appetizers take on a different dimension by serving to heighten anticipation of what's to come. It becomes more important for appetizers to showcase richness and variety in meat-based dishes for those on a carnivorous diet, so that the very beginning of the meal comes out in line with the dietary preference.

The next chapter contains a myriad of appetizers sure to please both meat-eaters and non-meat-eaters. These dishes showcase how versatile meat, eggs, and low-lactose dairy really are by incorporating simple, high quality ingredients that deliver flavor. Whether you're entertaining during a holiday or just making a festive meal for your family, these appetizers will set the stage for a truly memorable—and meaty—feast.

From the crackly, salty bacon-wrapped scallops to the creamy, buttery chicken liver pâté, these appetizers will surely tempt your guests and get their taste buds in gear for the further hearty dishes. Each dish is not only delicious but also adheres strictly to the principles of the carnivore diet, hence making it easier for one to stick to while enjoying the festive season.

Let's dive into these recipes and make the beginning of your holiday meal off right!

BACON-WRAPPED SCALLOPS

INGREDIENTS

12 LARGE SCALLOPS

12 SLICES OF BACON (STREAKY BACON)

SEA SALT

FRESHLY GROUND BLACK PEPPER

2 TBSP BUTTER (OPTIONAL FOR BASTING)

 METHOD BAKED

 TIME 25 MIN

 SERVING 4

DIFFICULTY EASY

METHOD

Oven-Baked and Broiled for a crisp finish on the bacon.

CALORIES	FAT	SATURATES	PROTEIN	CARBS	SUGARS	SALT	FIBER
320	24g	9g	25g	0g	0g	1.5g	0g

DIRECTIONS

STAGE I

1. Pat the scallops dry with paper towels to remove excess moisture.
2. Season the scallops lightly with sea salt and freshly ground black pepper.
3. Lay out the bacon slices on a clean surface.

STAGE II

1. Wrap each scallop with a slice of bacon, securing it with a toothpick if necessary. If the bacon slices are too long, trim them to fit around the scallops neatly.
2. Place the bacon-wrapped scallops on a baking sheet lined with parchment paper.
3. Bake in a preheated oven at 400°F (200°C) for 15-18 minutes, or until the bacon is almost crispy.
4. Switch the oven to broil (grill in the UK) for the last 2-3 minutes to crisp up the bacon further if needed.

CHICKEN LIVER PÂTÉ

INGREDIENTS

500G (1 LB) CHICKEN LIVERS, CLEANED
AND TRIMMED

100G (7 TBSP) BUTTER, DIVIDED

1 SMALL ONION, FINELY CHOPPED
(OPTIONAL, BASED ON PERSONAL
PREFERENCE)

2 CLOVES GARLIC, MINCED

100ML (3.5 FL OZ) HEAVY CREAM

SEA SALT

FRESHLY GROUND BLACK PEPPER

METHOD	TIME	SERVING	DIFFICULTY
SAUTÉED	30 MIN	6	MEDIUM

METHOD

Sautéed on the stovetop and blended until smooth.

CALORIES	FAT	SATURATES	PROTEIN	CARBS	SUGARS	SALT	FIBER
240	20g	12g	15g	1g	0g	0.8g	0g

DIRECTIONS

STAGE I

1. Clean and trim the chicken livers, removing any connective tissue.
2. Pat them dry with a paper towel.
3. Season the livers lightly with sea salt and freshly ground black pepper.

STAGE II

1. In a large skillet, melt 50g (3.5 tbsp) of butter over medium heat.
2. Add the chicken livers and sauté until they are browned on the outside and slightly pink on the inside, about 5 minutes.
3. Remove the livers from the pan and set aside. In the same pan, add the remaining butter, garlic, and onion (if using).
4. Sauté until softened.
5. Add the livers back to the pan, then pour in the heavy cream.
6. Simmer for another 2 minutes.
7. Transfer the mixture to a food processor and blend until smooth. Adjust seasoning to taste.

FESTIVE APPETIZERS

BEEF TARTARE

INGREDIENTS

400G (14 OZ) HIGH-QUALITY BEEF
TENDERLOIN, FINELY CHOPPED

2 EGG YOLKS

1 TBSP CAPERS, RINSED AND CHOPPED
(OPTIONAL)

1 TSP DIJON MUSTARD (OPTIONAL)

SEA SALT

FRESHLY GROUND BLACK PEPPER

1 TBSP FINELY CHOPPED SHALLOTS
(OPTIONAL)

	METHOD	TIME	SERVING	DIFFICULTY
	NONE	20 MIN	4	MEDIUM

METHOD

No cooking required; served raw.

CALORIES	FAT	SATURATES	PROTEIN	CARBS	SUGARS	SALT	FIBER
300	22g	8g	24g	1g	0g	1g	0g

DIRECTIONS

STAGE I

1. Finely chop the beef tenderloin using a sharp knife, ensuring the meat is cut into very small pieces.
2. In a bowl, mix the chopped beef with sea salt, freshly ground black pepper, capers, mustard, and shallots (if using).

STAGE II

1. Divide the seasoned beef mixture into four portions and shape each portion into a small, round patty.
2. Place each patty on a serving plate.
3. Make a small indentation in the center of each patty and carefully place an egg yolk into each indentation.

HARD CHEESE AND MEAT PLATTER

INGREDIENTS

200G (7 OZ) AGED CHEDDAR CHEESE,
SLICED

150G (5 OZ) HARD SALAMI, SLICED

150G (5 OZ) PROSCIUTTO, THINLY
SLICED

150G (5 OZ) CHORIZO, SLICED

SEA SALT (OPTIONAL, FOR SPRINKLING)

METHOD	**TIME**	**SERVING**	**DIFFICULTY**
NONE	30 MIN	4	EASY

METHOD

No cooking required; served cold.

CALORIES	FAT	SATURATES	PROTEIN	CARBS	SUGARS	SALT	FIBER
350	28g	12g	24g	0g	0g	1.5g	0g

DIRECTIONS

STAGE I

1. Slice the aged cheddar cheese into thin pieces.
2. Arrange the slices of hard salami, prosciutto, and chorizo on a large serving platter.

STAGE II

1. Place the sliced cheese on the platter alongside the meats.
2. Arrange the ingredients in a visually appealing manner, with the different meats and cheese types separated.
3. Sprinkle lightly with sea salt if desired.

GRILLED SHRIMP SKEWERS

INGREDIENTS

16 LARGE SHRIMP, PEELED AND
DEVEINED

2 TBSP OLIVE OIL

SEA SALT

FRESHLY GROUND BLACK PEPPER

1 TBSP LEMON JUICE (OPTIONAL)

METHOD	TIME	SERVING	DIFFICULTY
GRILLED	15 MIN	4	EASY

METHOD

Grilled on a medium-high heat grill or grill pan.

CALORIES	FAT	SATURATES	PROTEIN	CARBS	SUGARS	SALT	FIBER
150	7g	1g	19g	0g	0g	0.8g	0g

DIRECTIONS

STAGE I

1. Peel and devein the shrimp, then pat them dry with paper towels.
2. Toss the shrimp in olive oil, sea salt, and freshly ground black pepper.
3. If desired, add a squeeze of lemon juice for a touch of acidity.

STAGE II

1. Thread the shrimp onto skewers, making sure they are evenly spaced.
2. Preheat a grill or grill pan to medium-high heat.
3. Grill the shrimp for 2-3 minutes on each side, or until they are pink and opaque, with light grill marks.

PART III

HEARTY SOUPS AND STEWS

Nothing beats a warm bowl of soup or stew, really; it's such a soul food and tummy-filling kind of dish, great for the body, particularly in this cooler season almost within the vicinity. Soups and stews are perfect for a carnivore diet: nutrient-dense, rich, and totally satisfying for strict nutritional rules. Composed of entirely animal products, these dishes are full of tastes and are bursting with necessary nutrients to cater to a nutritious and comforting experience after each scoop.

This chapter is a selection of soups and stews that epitomizes the best in carnivore cooking. Easy recipes loaded with flavor from a few well-chosen ingredients like beef bones, chicken, pork belly, and lamb shanks. Whether you fancy a light, brothy soup or a hearty, slow-cooked stew, these recipes will hit the spot at festive mealtimes.

Let's dive into these warm dishes that are fabulous for sharing with friends and loved ones or curling up with on a cold winter's night.

BEEF BONE BROTH

INGREDIENTS

2 KG (4.4 LBS) BEEF BONES (MARROW, KNUCKLE, OR OXTAIL)

2 TBSP APPLE CIDER VINEGAR (OPTIONAL)

SEA SALT

FRESHLY GROUND BLACK PEPPER

3 LITERS (3 QUARTS) WATER

METHOD	**TIME**	**SERVING**	**DIFFICULTY**
SIMMERED	12 HR	8	EASY

METHOD
Slow simmered on the stovetop or in a slow cooker for deep, rich flavor.

CALORIES	FAT	SATURATES	PROTEIN	CARBS	SUGARS	SALT	FIBER
50	3g	1g	5g	0g	0g	0.5g	0g

DIRECTIONS

STAGE I

1. Place the beef bones in a large stockpot or slow cooker.
2. Pour in the water, ensuring the bones are fully submerged.
3. Add the apple cider vinegar, which helps extract minerals from the bones.
4. Season lightly with sea salt and freshly ground black pepper.

STAGE II

1. Bring the mixture to a gentle boil over medium heat, then reduce to a low simmer.
2. Skim off any foam that rises to the surface during the first hour of cooking.
3. Allow the broth to simmer for at least 12 hours, or up to 24 hours, adding more water if necessary to keep the bones submerged.
4. Strain the broth through a fine mesh sieve and adjust seasoning before serving.

CREAMY CHICKEN SOUP

INGREDIENTS

1 WHOLE CHICKEN (ABOUT 1.5 KG /
3.3 LBS), CUT INTO PIECES
1 LITER (1 QUART) CHICKEN BROTH
200 ML (7 FL OZ) HEAVY CREAM
50G (3.5 TBSP) BUTTER
SEA SALT
FRESHLY GROUND BLACK PEPPER

METHOD	TIME	SERVING	DIFFICULTY
SIMMERED	45 MIN	6	EASY

METHOD

Simmered on the stovetop for a rich, creamy texture.

CALORIES	FAT	SATURATES	PROTEIN	CARBS	SUGARS	SALT	FIBER
320	25g	14g	24g	1g	0g	1.2g	0g

DIRECTIONS

STAGE I

1. Cut the chicken into pieces and season lightly with sea salt and freshly ground black pepper.
2. Melt the butter in a large pot over medium heat.

STAGE II

1. Add the chicken pieces to the pot and cook until they are browned on all sides.
2. Pour in the chicken broth, bringing the mixture to a boil.
3. Reduce the heat and let it simmer for 30 minutes, until the chicken is cooked through.
4. Remove the chicken pieces, shred the meat, and return it to the pot.
5. Stir in the heavy cream and simmer for another 5 minutes until the soup is rich and creamy.

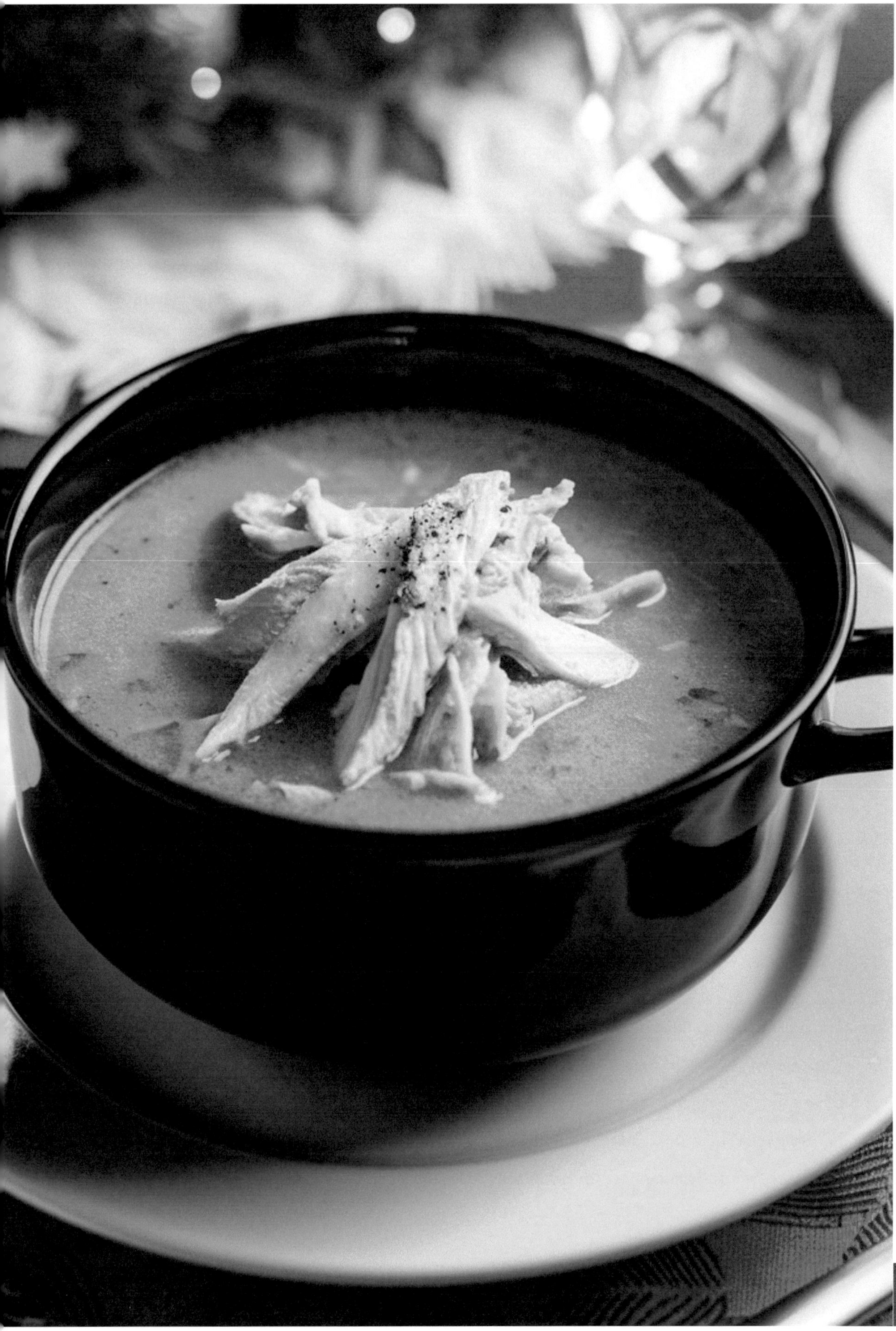

HEARTY SOUPS AND STEWS

PORK BELLY STEW

INGREDIENTS

1 KG (2.2 LBS) PORK BELLY, CUT INTO
LARGE CUBES

1 LITER (1 QUART) BONE BROTH (BEEF
OR PORK)

100 ML (3.5 FL OZ) HEAVY CREAM

SEA SALT

FRESHLY GROUND BLACK PEPPER

2 TBSP LARD OR TALLOW

METHOD	TIME	SERVING	DIFFICULTY
SLOW-COOKED	2 HR	6	MEDIUM

METHOD

Slow-cooked on the stovetop for tender, flavorful meat.

CALORIES	FAT	SATURATES	PROTEIN	CARBS	SUGARS	SALT	FIBER
450	40g	18g	20g	0g	0g	1g	0g

DIRECTIONS

STAGE I

1. Cut the pork belly into large cubes and season with sea salt and freshly ground black pepper.
2. Heat the lard or tallow in a large pot over medium heat.

STAGE II

1. Add the pork belly cubes to the pot and brown them on all sides.
2. Pour in the bone broth and bring the mixture to a boil.
3. Reduce the heat to a low simmer and cover the pot.
4. Cook for 1.5 hours, until the pork belly is tender.
5. Stir in the heavy cream and simmer for an additional 10 minutes, allowing the flavors to meld together.

LAMB SHANK STEW

INGREDIENTS

4 LAMB SHANKS

1.5 LITERS (1.5 QUARTS) BEEF OR LAMB BROTH

100G (7 TBSP) BUTTER

SEA SALT

FRESHLY GROUND BLACK PEPPER

1 TBSP FRESH ROSEMARY, CHOPPED (OPTIONAL)

METHOD	**TIME**	**SERVING**	**DIFFICULTY**
SLOW-COOKED	3 HR	4	MEDIUM

METHOD

Slow-cooked on the stovetop for tender, flavorful lamb.

CALORIES	FAT	SATURATES	PROTEIN	CARBS	SUGARS	SALT	FIBER
600	45g	20g	45g	0g	0g	1.2g	0g

DIRECTIONS

STAGE I

1. Season the lamb shanks generously with sea salt and freshly ground black pepper.
2. In a large pot, melt the butter over medium heat.

STAGE II

1. Add the lamb shanks to the pot and brown them on all sides.
2. Pour in the broth and add the chopped rosemary, if using.
3. Bring the mixture to a boil, then reduce the heat to low and cover the pot.
4. Simmer the stew for 2.5 hours, until the lamb is tender and falling off the bone.
5. Adjust seasoning before serving.

FISH BROTH WITH SARDINES

INGREDIENTS

500G (1.1 LBS) WHITE FISH (COD OR HADDOCK)

2 CANS SARDINES IN OIL, DRAINED

1 LITER (1 QUART) FISH STOCK

100 ML (3.5 FL OZ) HEAVY CREAM

SEA SALT

FRESHLY GROUND BLACK PEPPER

METHOD	TIME	SERVING	DIFFICULTY
SIMMERED	1 HR	4	EASY

METHOD

Simmered on the stovetop for a rich, flavorful broth.

CALORIES	FAT	SATURATES	PROTEIN	CARBS	SUGARS	SALT	FIBER
280	20g	10g	22g	0g	0g	1.5g	0g

DIRECTIONS

STAGE I

1. Cut the white fish into large chunks and drain the sardines.
2. Season the fish with sea salt and freshly ground black pepper.

STAGE II

1. In a large pot, bring the fish stock to a gentle simmer.
2. Add the chunks of white fish and cook until the fish is tender, about 20 minutes.
3. Add the sardines and heavy cream, stirring gently to combine.
4. Simmer for an additional 10 minutes, allowing the flavors to meld together.
5. Adjust seasoning before serving.

PART IV

SHOW-STOPPING
MAIN COURSES

A main course is often the crowning glory of every holiday feast—a dish from which all other people collect around and look forward to. In a carnivore diet, the main course assumes a bigger function since it's the richness, flavor, and versatility in meat. Whether you're having a large Christmas dinner or just a smaller, more laid-back gathering, these show-stopping main courses are sure to please your guests and give them a filling, festive meal.

In this chapter, you will find recipes representing the finest cuts of meat, cooked to perfection with simple yet powerful seasonings. These dishes will help to praise the real taste present in good quality meats by applying techniques which truly bring out the potential that each cut bears. From succulent prime rib to golden-brown turkey, these recipes will help you ensure that your holiday feast will be truly unforgettable.

Now, let's dive into those centerpiece-worthy dishes that are sure to be the high point of your carnivore Christmas table.

ROAST PRIME RIB

INGREDIENTS

2.5 KG (5.5 LBS) PRIME RIB ROAST,
BONE-IN

2 TBSP SEA SALT

1 TBSP FRESHLY GROUND BLACK PEPPER

2 TBSP BUTTER, SOFTENED

METHOD

ROASTED

TIME

2.5 HR

SERVING

6

DIFFICULTY

MEDIUM

METHOD

Roasted in the oven for a perfectly tender and flavorful prime rib.

CALORIES	FAT	SATURATES	PROTEIN	CARBS	SUGARS	SALT	FIBER
650	52g	24g	45g	0g	0g	1.8g	0g

DIRECTIONS

STAGE I

1. Remove the prime rib from the refrigerator and allow it to come to room temperature.
2. Preheat the oven to 475°F (245°C).
3. Season the roast generously with sea salt and freshly ground black pepper.
4. Rub the softened butter all over the surface of the roast.

STAGE II

1. Place the prime rib on a roasting rack in a large roasting pan.
2. Roast in the preheated oven for 15 minutes, then reduce the temperature to 325°F (165°C) and continue roasting for about 2 hours, or until the internal temperature reaches 130°F (54°C) for medium-rare.
3. Remove the roast from the oven, tent with foil, and let it rest for 20 minutes before carving.

SHOW-STOPPING MAIN COURSES

GLAZED HAM (CARNIVORE STYLE)

INGREDIENTS

3 KG (6.6 LBS) BONE-IN HAM

500 ML (2 CUPS) BONE BROTH

50G (3.5 TBSP) BUTTER

1 TSP SEA SALT

1 TSP FRESHLY GROUND BLACK PEPPER

METHOD	TIME	SERVING	DIFFICULTY
ROASTED	3 HR	8	MEDIUM

METHOD

Roasted in the oven with a rich, buttery glaze for a tender, flavorful ham.

CALORIES	FAT	SATURATES	PROTEIN	CARBS	SUGARS	SALT	FIBER
350	25g	12g	30g	0g	0g	2.2g	0g

DIRECTIONS

STAGE I

1. Preheat the oven to 325°F (165°C).
2. Place the ham in a large roasting pan. In a small saucepan, melt the butter and mix it with the bone broth, sea salt, and freshly ground black pepper.

STAGE II

1. Pour the butter and bone broth mixture over the ham, ensuring it is well coated.
2. Cover the ham with foil and bake for 2 hours.
3. Remove the foil and baste the ham with the pan juices.
4. Increase the oven temperature to 375°F (190°C) and bake for an additional 30 minutes, or until the glaze is golden and slightly caramelized.

ROAST TURKEY WITH HERB BUTTER

INGREDIENTS

1 WHOLE TURKEY (5 KG / 11 LBS), THAWED

200G (7 TBSP) BUTTER, SOFTENED

2 TBSP SEA SALT

1 TBSP FRESHLY GROUND BLACK PEPPER

2 TBSP FRESH ROSEMARY, FINELY CHOPPED

2 TBSP FRESH THYME, FINELY CHOPPED

METHOD	TIME	SERVING	DIFFICULTY
ROASTED	3.5 HR	8	MEDIUM

METHOD

Roasted in the oven with herb-infused butter for a golden, flavorful turkey.

CALORIES	FAT	SATURATES	PROTEIN	CARBS	SUGARS	SALT	FIBER
480	35g	16g	40g	0g	0g	1.6g	0g

DIRECTIONS

STAGE I

1. Preheat the oven to 325°F (165°C).
2. Pat the turkey dry with paper towels. In a small bowl, mix the softened butter with the chopped rosemary, thyme, sea salt, and freshly ground black pepper.
3. Rub the herb butter mixture all over the turkey, including under the skin for extra flavor.

STAGE II

1. Place the turkey on a roasting rack in a large roasting pan.
2. Roast in the preheated oven for about 3 hours, or until the internal temperature in the thickest part of the thigh reaches 165°F (75°C).
3. Baste the turkey with the pan juices every 30 minutes.
4. Once cooked, remove the turkey from the oven, tent with foil, and let it rest for 20 minutes before carving.

RACK OF LAMB

INGREDIENTS

2 RACKS OF LAMB (ABOUT 1.2 KG / 2.6 LBS TOTAL)

2 TBSP SEA SALT

1 TBSP FRESHLY GROUND BLACK PEPPER

2 TBSP BUTTER, MELTED

1 TBSP FRESH ROSEMARY, CHOPPED

1 TBSP FRESH THYME, CHOPPED

METHOD	TIME	SERVING	DIFFICULTY
ROASTED	1.5 HR	4	MEDIUM

METHOD

Roasted in the oven with a herb butter crust for a tender, flavorful lamb.

CALORIES	FAT	SATURATES	PROTEIN	CARBS	SUGARS	SALT	FIBER
550	45g	20g	30g	0g	0g	1.4g	0g

DIRECTIONS

STAGE I

1. Preheat the oven to 400°F (200°C).
2. Season the lamb racks generously with sea salt and freshly ground black pepper.
3. In a small bowl, mix the melted butter with the chopped rosemary and thyme.

STAGE II

1. Place the lamb racks on a roasting tray, fat side up.
2. Brush the herb butter mixture over the lamb.
3. Roast in the preheated oven for 25-30 minutes, or until the internal temperature reaches 130°F (54°C) for medium-rare.
4. Remove from the oven and let the lamb rest for 10 minutes before slicing into individual chops.

CARNIVORE MEATLOAF

INGREDIENTS

---

1 KG (2.2 LBS) GROUND BEEF

200G (7 OZ) HARD CHEESE, GRATED

4 LARGE EGGS

50G (3.5 TBSP) BUTTER, MELTED

SEA SALT

FRESHLY GROUND BLACK PEPPER

METHOD

BAKED

TIME

1.5 HR

SERVING

6

DIFFICULTY

EASY

METHOD

Baked in the oven for a hearty, cheesy meatloaf.

CALORIES	FAT	SATURATES	PROTEIN	CARBS	SUGARS	SALT	FIBER
520	42g	18g	35g	0g	0g	1.6g	0g

DIRECTIONS

STAGE I

1. Preheat the oven to 350°F (175°C).

2. In a large bowl, combine the ground beef, grated cheese, eggs, melted butter, sea salt, and freshly ground black pepper.

3. Mix thoroughly until all ingredients are evenly incorporated.

STAGE II

1. Transfer the mixture into a loaf pan, pressing it down evenly.

2. Place the loaf pan on a baking tray and bake in the preheated oven for 1 hour, or until the meatloaf is cooked through and the top is golden brown.

3. Allow the meatloaf to rest for 10 minutes before slicing and serving.

PART V

FESTIVE SIDES

Although the main course is usually the star of most meals, the side dishes are equally as important in creating a memorable meal. When it comes to pure carnivore feasting, every single part of the meal—including the sides—needs to play by the same rules. Here's a small selection of the best side dishes, equally tasty and compliant, that can form a bright backdrop to your carnivore cook-ups and offer the perfect companions to your larger holiday show-stopper dishes.

They are rich and very tasty side dishes—very satisfying, made with animal products only, such as butter, cheese, eggs, and various cuts of meat. Such recipes serve well those who just want a little variety on their plate or go all out with that richness of a carnivore's cook.

Join us as we explore these side dishes that will go with your carnivorous Christmas meal—making certain that each bite is as delightful as the last.

BUTTER-BASTED SHRIMP

INGREDIENTS

16 LARGE SHRIMP, PEELED AND
DEVEINED
100G (7 TBSP) BUTTER
SEA SALT
FRESHLY GROUND BLACK PEPPER

METHOD	TIME	SERVING	DIFFICULTY
SAUTÉED	15 MIN	4	EASY

METHOD

Sautéed in butter for a rich, flavorful dish.

CALORIES	FAT	SATURATES	PROTEIN	CARBS	SUGARS	SALT	FIBER
250	20g	12g	18g	0g	0g	1.2g	0g

DIRECTIONS

STAGE I

1. Melt the butter in a large skillet over medium heat.
2. Season the shrimp with sea salt and freshly ground black pepper.

STAGE II

1. Add the shrimp to the skillet and cook until they are pink and opaque, basting them with the melted butter as they cook.
2. Remove from the skillet and serve immediately, drizzling the remaining butter over the top.

CHEESY EGG BAKE

INGREDIENTS

8 LARGE EGGS

200G (7 OZ) HARD CHEESE, GRATED

100ML (3.5 FL OZ) HEAVY CREAM

50G (3.5 TBSP) BUTTER, MELTED

SEA SALT

FRESHLY GROUND BLACK PEPPER

 METHOD
BAKED

 TIME
40 MIN

SERVING
6

 DIFFICULTY
EASY

METHOD

Baked in the oven for a rich, cheesy texture.

CALORIES	FAT	SATURATES	PROTEIN	CARBS	SUGARS	SALT	FIBER
320	28g	15g	18g	1g	0g	1.3g	0g

DIRECTIONS

STAGE I

1. Preheat the oven to 350°F (175°C).
2. In a large bowl, whisk together the eggs, grated cheese, heavy cream, melted butter, sea salt, and freshly ground black pepper.

STAGE II

1. Pour the mixture into a greased baking dish.
2. Bake in the preheated oven for 30 minutes, or until the top is golden brown and the eggs are set.
3. Allow to cool slightly before slicing and serving.

CARNIVORE SAUSAGE ROLLS

INGREDIENTS

500G (1.1 LBS) GROUND BEEF

500G (1.1 LBS) GROUND PORK

12 SLICES OF BACON

200G (7 OZ) HARD CHEESE, GRATED

SEA SALT

FRESHLY GROUND BLACK PEPPER

METHOD	TIME	SERVING	DIFFICULTY
BAKED	1 HR	6	MEDIUM

METHOD

Baked in the oven for a crispy, savory dish.

CALORIES	FAT	SATURATES	PROTEIN	CARBS	SUGARS	SALT	FIBER
600	50g	20g	35g	0g	0g	2g	0g

DIRECTIONS

STAGE I

1. Preheat the oven to 375°F (190°C).
2. In a large bowl, mix together the ground beef, ground pork, grated cheese, sea salt, and freshly ground black pepper.

STAGE II

1. Divide the meat mixture into 12 equal portions and shape each into a log.
2. Wrap each log with a slice of bacon, securing with a toothpick if necessary.
3. Place the sausage rolls on a baking sheet lined with parchment paper.
4. Bake in the preheated oven for 30-35 minutes, or until the bacon is crispy and the sausage is cooked through.

STUFFED PORK LOIN

INGREDIENTS

1.5 KG (3.3 LBS) PORK LOIN

500G (1.1 LBS) GROUND PORK

200G (7 OZ) HARD CHEESE, GRATED

2 TBSP BUTTER, MELTED

SEA SALT

FRESHLY GROUND BLACK PEPPER

METHOD	TIME	SERVING	DIFFICULTY
ROASTED	2 HR	6	MEDIUM

METHOD

Roasted in the oven for a juicy, flavorful main dish.

CALORIES	FAT	SATURATES	PROTEIN	CARBS	SUGARS	SALT	FIBER
700	55g	25g	50g	0g	0g	2.5g	0g

DIRECTIONS

STAGE I

1. Preheat the oven to 350°F (175°C).
2. Butterfly the pork loin by slicing it lengthwise, being careful not to cut all the way through.
3. In a bowl, mix together the ground pork, grated cheese, melted butter, sea salt, and freshly ground black pepper.

STAGE II

1. Spread the stuffing mixture evenly over the opened pork loin.
2. Roll the pork loin tightly and secure it with kitchen twine.
3. Place the stuffed pork loin in a roasting pan and roast in the preheated oven for 1.5 hours, or until the internal temperature reaches 145°F (63°C).
4. Let the pork loin rest for 10 minutes before slicing and serving.

FESTIVE SIDES

45

BEEF FAT ROASTED BONES

INGREDIENTS

1 KG (2.2 LBS) MARROW BONES

200G (7 OZ) BEEF FAT OR TALLOW

SEA SALT

FRESHLY GROUND BLACK PEPPER

METHOD	TIME	SERVING	DIFFICULTY
ROASTED	1.5 HR	4	EASY

METHOD

Roasted in the oven for rich, flavorful marrow.

CALORIES	FAT	SATURATES	PROTEIN	CARBS	SUGARS	SALT	FIBER
450	40g	20g	15g	0g	0g	1g	0g

DIRECTIONS

STAGE I

1. Preheat the oven to 400°F (200°C).
2. Place the marrow bones in a large roasting pan.
3. Rub the beef fat or tallow over the bones, coating them evenly.
4. Season with sea salt and freshly ground black pepper.

STAGE II

1. Roast the bones in the preheated oven for 45 minutes to 1 hour, or until the marrow is soft and the bones are browned and crispy on the outside.
2. Serve hot, with the marrow scooped out and spread on a slice of grilled steak or enjoyed on its own.

PART VI

DELECTABLE

DESSERTS

Desserts are likely to be a meal's highlight and, during the holiday time, a special place at the table. Traditional sweet treats are off-limits for anyone following a carnivore diet, which in no way means you have to do without indulgent and seasonal dessert options. This chapter will introduce you to a collection of sweet-like treats fitting the holidays that will be in complete agreement with a carnivore diet, giving you a satisfying and tasty end to your holiday meal.

These recipes take rich, creamy ingredients like butter, cream, and eggs and transform them into beautiful desserts befitting of a celebration. Whether you need a show-stopping cheesecake or just a simple yet satisfying fat bomb, these treats will surely be a hit at your carnivore Christmas feast.

Now, let's dive into these scrumptious desserts that will round out your holiday meal without bending your carnivore diet one bit.

CARNIVORE CHEESECAKE

INGREDIENTS

200G (7 OZ) PORK RINDS, GROUND INTO
CRUMBS

100G (7 TBSP) BUTTER, MELTED

400G (14 OZ) CREAM CHEESE, SOFTENED

200ML (7 FL OZ) HEAVY CREAM

3 LARGE EGGS

1 TSP VANILLA EXTRACT (OPTIONAL)

SEA SALT

METHOD	TIME	SERVING	DIFFICULTY
BAKED	4 HR	8	MEDIUM

METHOD
Baked in the oven for a rich, creamy texture.

CALORIES	FAT	SATURATES	PROTEIN	CARBS	SUGARS	SALT	FIBER
450	40g	25g	15g	2g	1g	1g	0g

DIRECTIONS

STAGE I

1. Preheat the oven to 350°F (175°C).
2. In a bowl, mix the ground pork rinds with melted butter and a pinch of sea salt.
3. Press the mixture into the bottom of a springform pan to form the crust.
4. Bake in the preheated oven for 10 minutes, then set aside to cool.

STAGE II

1. In a large bowl, beat the cream cheese until smooth.
2. Add the heavy cream, eggs, vanilla extract (if using), and a pinch of sea salt, mixing until fully combined.
3. Pour the filling over the cooled crust and smooth the top.
4. Bake in the preheated oven for 50 minutes, or until the center is just set.
5. Let the cheesecake cool to room temperature, then refrigerate for at least 3 hours before serving.

EGGNOG PUDDING

INGREDIENTS

8 EGG YOLKS

200ML (7 FL OZ) HEAVY CREAM

50G (3.5 TBSP) BUTTER

1 TSP VANILLA EXTRACT (OPTIONAL)

SEA SALT

GROUND NUTMEG (OPTIONAL)

METHOD	TIME	SERVING	DIFFICULTY
WHISK	30 MIN	4	EASY

METHOD

Cooked on the stovetop and chilled for a creamy, festive treat.

CALORIES	FAT	SATURATES	PROTEIN	CARBS	SUGARS	SALT	FIBER
300	28g	16g	8g	1g	0g	0.5g	0g

DIRECTIONS

STAGE I

1. In a medium saucepan, whisk together the egg yolks, heavy cream, butter, vanilla extract (if using), and a pinch of sea salt.
2. Cook over low heat, stirring constantly, until the mixture thickens and coats the back of a spoon.

STAGE II

1. Pour the mixture into individual serving dishes.
2. Sprinkle with ground nutmeg, if desired.
3. Refrigerate for at least 2 hours before serving.

BUTTER AND CHEESE FAT BOMBS

INGREDIENTS

100G (7 TBSP) BUTTER, SOFTENED

100G (7 OZ) AGED HARD CHEESE, GRATED

SEA SALT

METHOD	TIME	SERVING	DIFFICULTY
NONE	15 MIN	10	EASY

METHOD

No cooking required; chilled for a satisfying, high-fat snack.

CALORIES	FAT	SATURATES	PROTEIN	CARBS	SUGARS	SALT	FIBER
150	14g	9g	5g	0g	0g	0.8g	0g

DIRECTIONS

STAGE I

1. In a bowl, combine the softened butter, grated cheese, and a pinch of sea salt.
2. Mix until smooth and well combined.

STAGE II

1. Roll the mixture into small balls and place them on a parchment-lined tray.
2. Refrigerate for at least 30 minutes to firm up before serving.

FROZEN CREAM BITES

INGREDIENTS

200ML (7 FL OZ) HEAVY CREAM

50G (3.5 TBSP) BUTTER, MELTED

SEA SALT

METHOD	TIME	SERVING	DIFFICULTY
NONE	10 MIN	10	EASY

METHOD

No cooking required; frozen for a cool, creamy treat.

CALORIES	FAT	SATURATES	PROTEIN	CARBS	SUGARS	SALT	FIBER
130	14g	9g	1g	0g	0g	0.4g	0g

DIRECTIONS

STAGE I

1. In a bowl, whisk together the heavy cream, melted butter, and a pinch of sea salt until smooth..

STAGE II

1. Pour the mixture into silicone molds or ice cube trays.
2. Freeze for at least 2 hours, or until solid.
3. Pop the frozen bites out of the molds and store them in an airtight container in the freezer.

CARNIVORE CUSTARD

INGREDIENTS

6 LARGE EGGS

200ML (7 FL OZ) HEAVY CREAM

50G (3.5 TBSP) HARD CHEESE, GRATED

1 TSP VANILLA EXTRACT (OPTIONAL)

SEA SALT

METHOD	TIME	SERVING	DIFFICULTY
BAKED	40 MIN	4	EASY

METHOD

Baked in a water bath for a smooth, creamy texture.

CALORIES	FAT	SATURATES	PROTEIN	CARBS	SUGARS	SALT	FIBER
320	28g	16g	12g	1g	0g	0.8g	0g

DIRECTIONS

STAGE I

1. Preheat the oven to 325°F (165°C).
2. In a large bowl, whisk together the eggs, heavy cream, grated cheese, vanilla extract (if using), and a pinch of sea salt.

STAGE II

1. Pour the mixture into a baking dish or individual ramekins.
2. Place the dish in a larger baking pan and fill the pan with hot water to reach halfway up the sides of the baking dish.
3. Bake in the preheated oven for 30 minutes, or until the custard is set but still slightly wobbly in the center.
4. Let the custard cool to room temperature before serving.

PART VII

CARNIVORE-FRIENDLY BEVERAGES

While on a carnivorous diet, one needs drinks that not only quench one's thirst but also feature on the diet. Most conventional drinks are taboo, though there are still many rich and nourishing options remaining. In this chapter, we will examine some friendly beverages on the carnivore diet that are easy to prepare and really satisfying to enjoy any time of the year—not just through the holidays.

From savory broths to creamy shakes, these beverages are crafted to give you comfort, warmth, and flavor as they keep you fully compliant with your carnivore way of life. Whether you need a morning pick-me-up, a festive drink, or a soothing evening beverage to help you unwind, these recipes have got your back.

Now, let's dive headfirst into these drinks that will keep you warm, nourished, and satisfied throughout this festive season.

BONE BROTH LATTE

INGREDIENTS

250ML (1 CUP) BONE BROTH (BEEF OR CHICKEN)

50ML (3.5 TBSP) HEAVY CREAM

1 TBSP BUTTER

SEA SALT (OPTIONAL)

METHOD	TIME	SERVING	DIFFICULTY
SIMMERED	10 MIN	1	EASY

METHOD

Simmered and blended for a rich, frothy beverage.

CALORIES	FAT	SATURATES	PROTEIN	CARBS	SUGARS	SALT	FIBER
200	18g	12g	5g	0g	0g	0.6g	0g

DIRECTIONS

STAGE I

1. In a small saucepan, heat the bone broth over medium heat until it begins to simmer.
2. Add the heavy cream and butter, stirring until the butter is fully melted and the mixture is well combined.

STAGE II

1. Transfer the mixture to a blender and blend on high for 30 seconds until frothy.
2. Pour into a mug and season with a pinch of sea salt if desired. Serve immediately.

CARNIVORE EGGNOG

INGREDIENTS

6 EGG YOLKS

400ML (14 FL OZ) HEAVY CREAM

100ML (3.5 FL OZ) MILK (OPTIONAL,
DEPENDING ON TOLERANCE)

1 TSP VANILLA EXTRACT (OPTIONAL)

1/2 TSP GROUND NUTMEG

SEA SALT

METHOD	TIME	SERVING	DIFFICULTY
WHISK	20 MIN	4	MEDIUM

METHOD

Cooked gently on the stovetop and chilled for a creamy, festive drink.

CALORIES	FAT	SATURATES	PROTEIN	CARBS	SUGARS	SALT	FIBER
400	35g	22g	8g	2g	1g	0.7g	0g

DIRECTIONS

STAGE I

1. In a medium saucepan, whisk together the egg yolks, heavy cream, milk (if using), vanilla extract (if using), ground nutmeg, and a pinch of sea salt.
2. Cook over low heat, stirring constantly, until the mixture thickens slightly and coats the back of a spoon.

STAGE II

1. Remove the saucepan from the heat and let the eggnog cool to room temperature.
2. Refrigerate for at least 2 hours to chill. Serve cold, with an extra sprinkle of nutmeg on top.

BUTTER COFFEE

INGREDIENTS

250ML (1 CUP) FRESHLY BREWED BLACK
COFFEE

2 TBSP BUTTER

SEA SALT (OPTIONAL)

METHOD
BLENDED

TIME
5 MIN

SERVING
1

DIFFICULTY
EASY

METHOD

Blended for a rich, creamy coffee.

CALORIES	FAT	SATURATES	PROTEIN	CARBS	SUGARS	SALT	FIBER
200	22g	14g	0g	0g	0g	0.2g	0g

DIRECTIONS

STAGE I

1. Brew a fresh cup of black coffee.
2. Add the butter to the hot coffee.

STAGE II

1. Transfer the coffee and butter mixture to a blender.
2. Blend on high for 30 seconds until frothy.
3. Pour into a mug and add a pinch of sea salt if desired. Serve immediately.

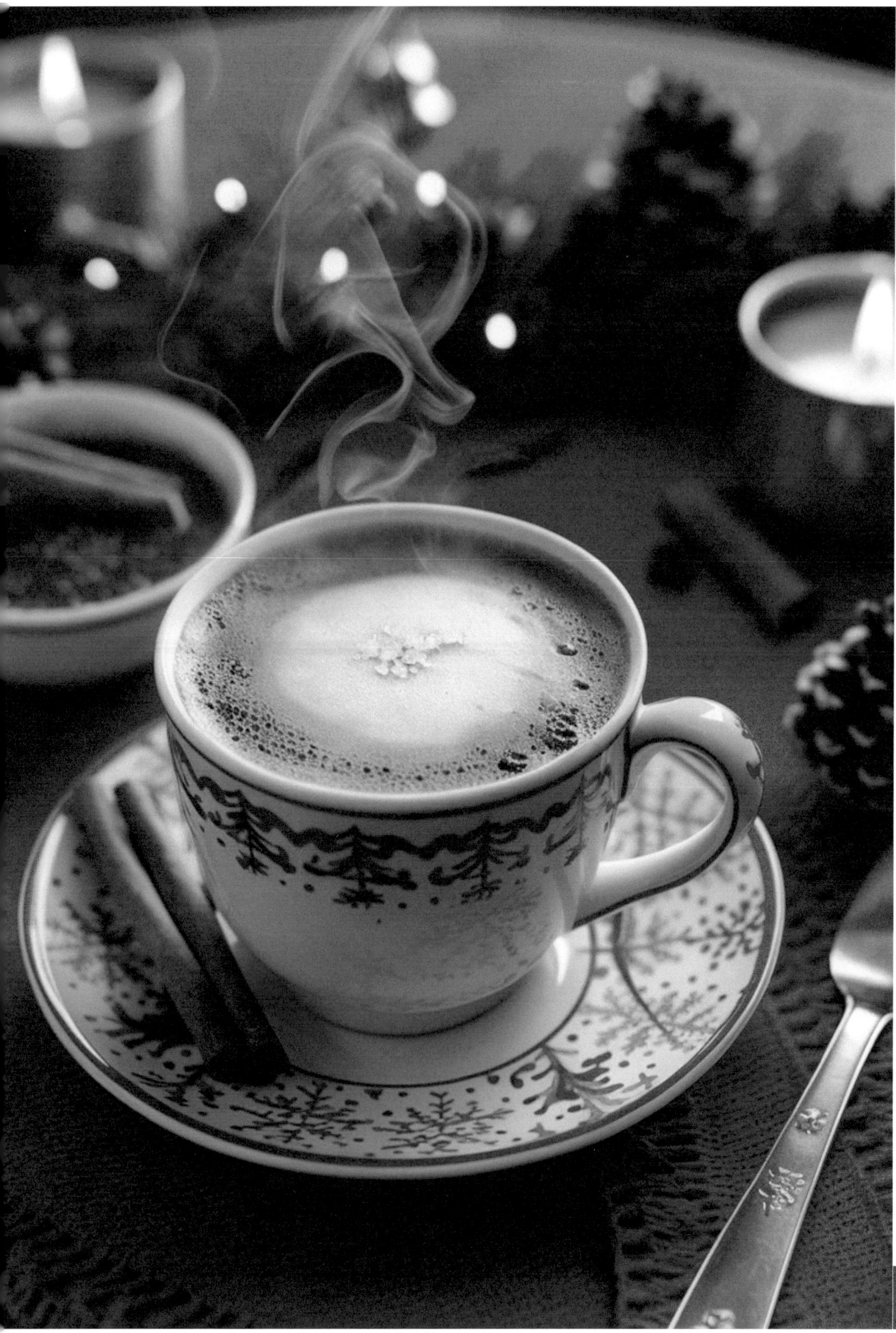

CARNIVORE-FRIENDLY BEVERAGES

CARNIVORE MILKSHAKE

INGREDIENTS

200ML (7 FL OZ) HEAVY CREAM

2 LARGE EGG YOLKS

1 TBSP BUTTER, MELTED

1 TSP VANILLA EXTRACT (OPTIONAL)

METHOD	TIME	SERVING	DIFFICULTY
BLENDED	10 MIN	1	EASY

METHOD

Blended for a thick, creamy shake.

CALORIES	FAT	SATURATES	PROTEIN	CARBS	SUGARS	SALT	FIBER
350	32g	18g	6g	1g	0g	0.3g	0g

DIRECTIONS

STAGE I

1. In a blender, combine the heavy cream, egg yolks, melted butter, and vanilla extract (if using).
2. Blend on high until the mixture is smooth and thick.

STAGE II

1. Pour the milkshake into a chilled glass.
2. Serve immediately.

MEAT STOCK TEA

INGREDIENTS

250ML (1 CUP) MEAT STOCK (BEEF OR CHICKEN)

SEA SALT

METHOD
SIMMERED

TIME
10 MIN

SERVING
1

DIFFICULTY
EASY

METHOD

Simmered and served hot for a simple, nourishing drink.

CALORIES	FAT	SATURATES	PROTEIN	CARBS	SUGARS	SALT	FIBER
50	2g	1g	8g	0g	0g	0.6g	0g

DIRECTIONS

STAGE I

1. Heat the meat stock in a small saucepan over medium heat until it begins to simmer.

STAGE II

1. Pour the hot stock into a mug.
2. Season with a pinch of sea salt if desired. Serve immediately.

PART VIII

CONCLUSION

TIPS FOR TRAVELING DURING THE HOLIDAYS

1. Plan Ahead: Before you travel, research your destination and identify places where you can find carnivore-friendly meals or ingredients. Pack a cooler with pre-cooked meats, hard cheese, and boiled eggs for snacks on the go.

2. Pack Essential Tools: Consider bringing portable cooking tools such as a mini grill or a small skillet, which can help you prepare meat-based meals wherever you are.

3. Stay Hydrated: Traveling can be dehydrating, so make sure to drink plenty of water and consider carrying some bone broth for added nourishment.

4. Snacks for the Road: Keep carnivore-friendly snacks on hand, such as beef jerky, pork rinds, or hard-boiled eggs, to avoid any temptation for non-carnivore foods.

5. Communicate Your Needs: If you're staying with family or friends, don't hesitate to communicate your dietary preferences in advance. Offer to bring your own food or contribute a carnivore dish to the meal.

CARNIVORE SHOPPING LIST

To ensure you're fully prepared for your carnivore holiday meals, here's a comprehensive shopping list of animal-based ingredients to keep on hand:

Meats and Seafood:

- Beef: Ribeye, prime rib, ground beef, beef liver, marrow bones
- Pork: Pork belly, pork loin, ground pork, bacon
- Poultry: Whole chicken, turkey, chicken liver, duck
- Lamb: Lamb shanks, rack of lamb, ground lamb
- Seafood: Shrimp, scallops, white fish (cod, haddock), sardines, salmon

Dairy:

- Cheese: Hard cheeses like cheddar, Parmesan, aged Gouda
- Butter: Unsalted butter, grass-fed if possible
- Cream: Heavy cream, sour cream

Eggs:

- Large eggs
- Egg yolks

Fats:

- Beef fat (tallow)
- Pork fat (lard)
- Duck fat
- Ghee (clarified butter)

Broths and Stocks:

- Bone broth (beef, chicken, or pork)
- Meat stock

Seasonings (Carnivore-Approved):

- Sea salt
- Freshly ground black pepper
- Fresh herbs (rosemary, thyme, sage)
- Dried spices (optional, like ground nutmeg for eggnog)

For those following a carnivore diet, it's important to have the right tools, books, and online resources to support your journey. Here are some recommendations:

Recommended Tools:

- Cast Iron Skillet: Ideal for searing meats to perfection.
- Slow Cooker: Great for making bone broths and slow-cooked meats.
- Meat Thermometer: Essential for ensuring meats are cooked to the right temperature.
- Food Processor: Useful for making ground meat or blending ingredients.
- Blender: Perfect for creating smooth, frothy carnivore drinks like bone broth lattes.

Recommended Books:

- **"The Carnivore Transition Diet for Beginners"** by Kimberly Stephens: This book is a great resource for anyone looking to transition into the carnivore diet, offering practical advice, meal plans, and recipes to make the switch as seamless as possible.

Online Resources:

- Carnivore Diet Forums: Join Discord communities of like-minded individuals where you can share experiences, tips, and recipes.

Scan QR Code to join:

Join Now

THANK YOU FOR CHOOSING **"CARNIVORE CHRISTMAS FEAST: DELICIOUS HOLIDAY RECIPES FOR A FESTIVE MEAT-BASED DIET."**

THIS BOOK WAS CREATED WITH THE INTENTION OF HELPING YOU CELEBRATE THE HOLIDAY SEASON WHILE STAYING TRUE TO THE CARNIVORE LIFESTYLE. WHETHER YOU'RE NEW TO THE CARNIVORE DIET OR HAVE BEEN FOLLOWING IT FOR SOME TIME, I HOPE THESE RECIPES, MEAL PLANS, AND TIPS BRING YOU JOY, NOURISHMENT, AND SATISFACTION DURING THIS SPECIAL TIME OF YEAR.

IF YOU ENJOYED THIS BOOK, I WOULD BE HONORED IF YOU LEFT A REVIEW ON AMAZON. YOUR FEEDBACK NOT ONLY HELPS OTHER READERS DISCOVER THIS BOOK, BUT IT ALSO HELPS ME IMPROVE AND CONTINUE CREATING CONTENT THAT SERVES YOU BETTER.

FOR THOSE OF YOU LOOKING TO CONTINUE OR DEEPEN YOUR CARNIVORE JOURNEY, I HIGHLY RECOMMEND CHECKING OUT MY PREVIOUS BOOK, "THE CARNIVORE TRANSITION DIET FOR BEGINNERS." IT OFFERS PRACTICAL ADVICE, MEAL PLANS, AND ADDITIONAL RECIPES TO SUPPORT YOU IN YOUR TRANSITION TO A FULLY CARNIVORE DIET.

THANK YOU AGAIN FOR YOUR SUPPORT, AND WE WISH YOU GREAT SUCCESS AND HEALTH ON YOUR CARNIVORE JOURNEY!

SINCERELY,

Kimberly Stephens